SOCCER

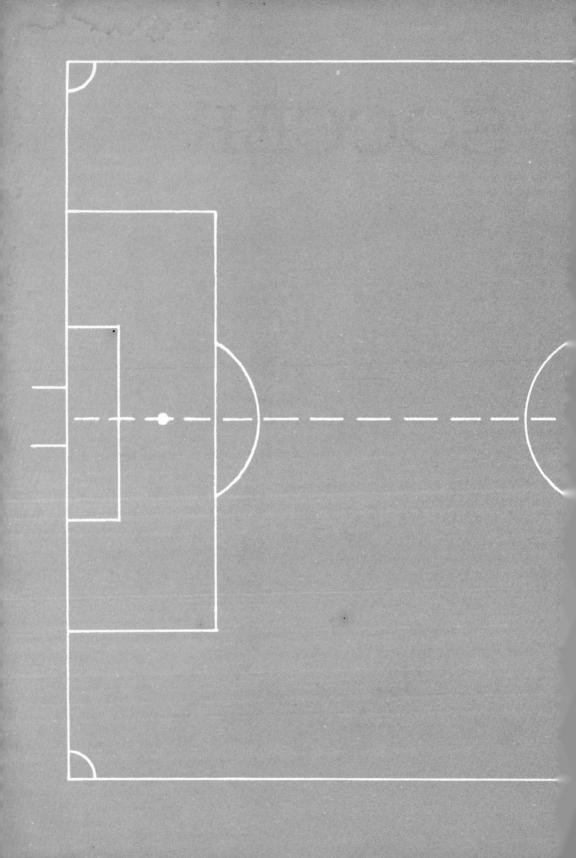

SOCCER

by HOWARD LISS

Foreword by
Sir Stanley Rous, C.B.E.

Illustrations by Harry Rosenbaum

HAWTHORN BOOKS, INC.
Publishers / New York

Library of Congress Catalog Card Number: 75–12144
ISBN: 0–8015–6910–9

Published by arrangement with T. Y. Crowell Company.

PHOTOGRAPHS: Asociación del Fútbol Argentino, 3, 16; Dallas Tornado Soccer Club (Jim Work, *Dallas Morning News*), 11; Detroit Soccer Co., Inc., 18; German Information Center (Bundesbildstelle), 15, (IN-Bild) 4, 19, 20, 24, 25; Golden Gate Gales, 10; Houston Sports Assn., Inc. (Gulf Photo), 2, 9, 13; New York Generals, National Professional Soccer League (Joao Luiz de Albuquerque), 21; New York Skyliners, United Soccer Assn., 1, 26, (Barton) 12; Real Federación Española de Fútbol (Alberto y Segovia), 8, 14, 17; UPI, 5, 6, 7, 22, 23.

Foreword

The new interest aroused by soccer in North America has become a subject for discussion wherever the game is played. The formation of new leagues in America, the acquisition of foreign players, the matches played throughout that continent during the summer of 1967 (with the help of teams from Europe and South America), have all made thousands of fans aware that more Americans are watching and playing soccer.

Naturally, many people who see good soccer for the first time, and who really become interested in it, will want a book to explain some of the incidents which occur during a match. Any book giving accurate information about the history and growth of the game, its worldwide popularity, and the regulations which govern it, is invaluable.

SOCCER is comprehensive in its survey of these subjects and will be useful to players and fans in school, college, university, or club, and to those unaffiliated individuals who just like the game. In the 1967 Pan American Games in Winnipeg, Canada, a special commentator helped novices to understand some of the duties, movements, skills, and decisions during the games. This book will serve a similar purpose.

Its pictures and diagrams have been carefully selected, and the frequent comparisons with other games, probably better known in North America, are clear and concise, and form a clever feature of the book.

I hope that SOCCER will find a place on the bookshelf of every player and supporter of the game.

Sir Stanley Rous, C.B.E.
President
Fédération Internationale de Football Association

Contents

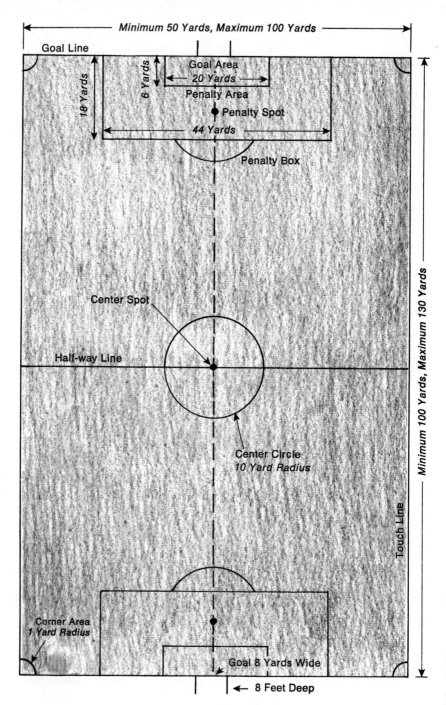

Minimum 50 Yards, Maximum 100 Yards

Goal Line

18 Yards

6 Yards

Goal Area
20 Yards

Penalty Area

Penalty Spot

44 Yards

Penalty Box

Center Spot

Half-way Line

Center Circle
10 Yard Radius

Minimum 100 Yards, Maximum 130 Yards

Touch Line

Corner Area
1 Yard Radius

Goal 8 Yards Wide

8 Feet Deep

THE SOCCER FIELD

I

This Game Called Soccer

In 1966, baseball's New York Yankees and professional football's New York Giants each finished last in their leagues during the same year. There was a good deal of moaning and muttering by hometown fans, and some sports writers made a few unkind remarks about the players and managers of both teams. But that was as far as things went. There was no rioting in the streets. There were no newspaper headlines denouncing Yankee manager Ralph Houk or Giant mentor Allie Sherman. In the New York State legislature, nobody said a word about the two clubs.

That same year the World Cup soccer matches were held in England. Teams from sixteen countries assembled to compete for the coveted Jules Rimet Trophy. The matches, held every four years, featured the greatest soccer players in the world, including Brazil's King Pelé, perhaps the highest paid athlete on Earth. Brazil, which had won the Cup twice in succession and needed only one more championship to retire the Trophy, was eliminated by a very strong Hungarian team. Italy, which had won two championships in a row during the 1930's, was put out by a lightly regarded squad from North Korea. The repercussions of both defeats were—to put it mildly—fantastic.

In Rio de Janeiro, grown men wept openly. In São Paulo, some misguided fan cried out "Long Live Hungary!" and the shout incited a riot that raged unchecked for hours. In Italy, one newspaper carried a huge headline "VERGOGNA! [Shame!]" Angry fans roamed the streets, denouncing manager Edmondo Fabbri and demanding he be hanged. In the Italian Parliament, two Socialist deputies made ranting speeches condemning the manager, the players, and the salaries they received. Meanwhile, England's Queen Elizabeth, who had rooted the British team to victory over West Germany, was smilingly presenting the Cup to the club's captain. The rest of England was celebrating as though it were V-E Day all over again. Pubs were opened ahead of time, Trafalgar Square was jammed with delirious people, and youngsters pranced around waving the Union Jack.

For almost a hundred years, soccer has had similar effects on its fans in nearly every nook and cranny of the world. The World Cup matches, considered the "World Series of Soccer," attracted rabid rooters from thousands of miles away. Prince Abdullah of Saudi Arabia, whose country did not enter the tournament, brought 25 players to London so that they could study the sport by watching the best teams in action. A network of radio and television stations broadcast the action to some 400,000,000 people in Europe, Asia,

Africa, and in North, Central and South America. Factory production dropped alarmingly during midweek games as fans stayed glued to television sets in homes and in store windows. Countless others walked the streets in a pose usually reserved for American teen-agers: one hand pressing a transistor radio close to the ear. A reporter in Spain stated flatly that soccer was ahead of bullfighting in popularity, at least in his country. Half a billion fans around the world forgot about politics, economic conditions, and family problems. Only one thing mattered—soccer!

Nobody seriously questions that soccer is the world's leading spectator sport. In England, where the game is a national habit like drinking tea, perhaps 2,000,000 fans pack the stadiums every Saturday afternoon from September through May. And, that same day, fans will flock to ball parks in Rio de Janeiro, Paris, Moscow, Bangkok, and many other cities. In the United States the great sports names are Mickey Mantle and Willy Mays; in the rest of the world the same hero-worship is accorded England's Bobby Charlton and Brazil's King Pelé.

What is there about this game of soccer that attracts so many fans? Why has it leaped across boundaries as no other sport has and probably as no other sport will? How come it doesn't attract as many fans in the United States as it does in other countries?

Soccer enthusiasts will tell you bluntly that their game has everything—speed, skill, drama, danger. It takes raw courage for a goalkeeper to dive headlong at an opposing player's feet as the ball shoots off the player's toe toward the net. Soccer demands outstanding physical conditioning, because everyone on the field, except the goalkeeper, is running almost constantly. Only when the ball goes over the touch line (out of bounds) is there a letup in the action. There are no time-out periods during the 45-minute halves, and substitutions are not allowed. Players are expected to run out the full 90 minutes of the game. How many men playing American football can do that?

Size doesn't mean a thing in soccer. A man, just 5½ feet tall and weighing 145 pounds, has the opportunity to outrun, outkick, outthink, outmaneuver, and outplay an opponent 6 inches taller and 50 pounds heavier. The small man can block out his bigger, heavier opponent, or leave him flat and foolish by dribbling through his legs.

Soccer is a simple game. There are fewer rules and regulations in it than in many other team sports. It's easier to understand and less cluttered up with complicated, meaningless trivia.

Spectators used to the American style of football tend to become impatient with a game that doesn't permit use of hands. Where, they might ask, is the pinpoint control of the ball that is so important in their own game? How about that accurate 50-yard pass from a quarterback to a cutting split end? Where is the timing that makes a fast hand-off so beautiful to watch? Why doesn't somebody just pick up that soccer ball and go busting through the field with it?

To answer the last question first, someone did pick up a soccer ball and that, more or less, was how the game of rugby got started. But that's another story about another game. As for control, accuracy, and timing, a good soccer player can do things with a ball, using only his head and feet, which are little short of incredible. A man like King Pelé can dribble with his feet just about as well as a professional basketball player can with his hands. A soccer pass, by means of the feet, is surprisingly accurate. And as for distance, most experts in American football have found that soccer stars can boot field goals as well as anybody. Think about the success of the Gogolak brothers with the Washington Redskins and the New York Giants.

Soccer, in some form or other, is one of the oldest sports known to mankind. The Chinese, about 2,500 years ago, played a game called *tsu chu*, which means "to kick a ball made of leather with the foot." The goals were bamboo poles, 10 feet high or more, with a silk net between them. The object of the game was to kick a ball, which was stuffed with hair, over the net or through a hole in it. Actually, the game was based on military strategy, using principles of attack and defense. The participants took it seriously, especially when playing before the emperor. The winners were handsomely rewarded with fruit, wine, silverware, and other gifts. The losing captain was flogged.

The British got their first taste of soccer from the invading Romans, who played a version of the game which they called *harpastum*. Teams would assemble on a field, and some kind of ball was thrown into their midst. Usually, it was the inflated bladder of an animal, which was kicked, pushed, shoved, and carried to a goal. That game bore little resemblance to modern soccer, but neither did any of the other early versions of the game.

There is a story about the origin of soccer in England and sports historians are fond of quoting it: in medieval times, the marauding Danes staged a raid on the town of Kingston, which was an Anglo-Saxon stronghold. The townspeople held out, fighting desperately, until help arrived from London and the Danes were beaten. The Danish general was killed, and his head cut off and kicked around the village in triumph. The incident happened on Shrove Tuesday, and thereafter, for years, the event was celebrated with a kicking game on that religious date. Perhaps the word "game" is not quite accurate. It resembled a riot more than anything else, with no particular rules or limitations. A ball, supplied by the local shoemaker, was kicked around the village, and the team getting it closest to the town meeting place was the winner. If the ball happened to fall into a river, the players went splashing in after it.

Another version of the same legend places this yearly event in the town of Chester. But that doesn't really matter, for there were peculiar things happening with soccer games in many other parts of the British Isles. In Midlothian, Scotland, soccer games of sorts were played between married women and spinsters, and the wedded females always beat the unmarried ones badly. They called the sport "melleys."

The British game of soccer (or "football") increased steadily in popularity, and soon it was played on other days besides holidays. This angered the English kings, because the game was distracting the stalwart young men from archery, and the army was suffering as a result. Some historians claim that the Anglo-Scottish War of 1297 wasn't taken seriously for a long time. It seems that several of King Edward's foot soldiers had lived in the English town of Lancaster, and they had a long, bitter rivalry with the Scots. They didn't want to kill off their old opponents; they wanted to play football against them.

In 1365, Edward III tried to put a stop to football by prohibiting the game completely. The trouble with the edict was that nobody could enforce it. Actually, it wasn't a game at all, but more like a parish fight. Everything was permissible: kicking, charging, tripping, hacking—as long as it wasn't out-and-out murder. It was possible to have 500 players to a team, and, because rules were varying, few of the players knew what they were doing. As late as the eighteenth century, one Frenchman watching this semi-organized brawl remarked, "If this is what Englishmen call playing, it would be impossible to describe what they would call fighting!" Yet the people loved every moment of it. So did many of the British peerage, especially Sir Walter Scott. Perhaps he saw in the game some of the jousting and mortal combat that was so vivid in his books.

It may be the Frenchman was unfamiliar with any form of football, but it is known that a version of the game was played along more organized lines in Florence and elsewhere in Italy during the sixteenth century. Some elements of the Italian game were brought to a school in Eton, England in 1624, upon the appointment of a new provost who had been an ambassador to Italy. This wasn't the first time football had been played in English schools. Harrow students were kicking a ball around as early as the year 1571. But now many schools began to play: Rugby, Winchester, Eton, and others. Each school made up rules to suit itself, and there were no standardized playing fields or number of men on a team. It was still a mob ballgame.

Slowly, order came from the chaos, sometimes with unforeseen results. For example, while some schools and amateur teams permitted the use of hands, most teams did not. In 1823 a young man attending Rugby School immortalized his name and started a new game. William Webb Ellis picked up the soccer ball during a game and ran with it. At first he was soundly rebuked, and the play was nullified by consent. But later some of the players decided that perhaps Ellis hadn't done such a bad thing after all, and his school decided to formulate a new rule: a player could run with the ball—carrying it—if the ball was received by a fair catch. Instead of being a villain, young Ellis was a hero. Today, on the boundary of the Rugby grounds is a tablet with this inscription: "This stone commemorates the exploit of William Webb Ellis, who, with a fine disregard for the rules of football as played in his time, first took the ball in his arms and ran with it, thus originating the distinctive feature of the Rugby game."

Perhaps this incident served to point up the need for a set of rules and regulations that would standardize soccer. In 1846 the first tentative steps toward that end were taken. Cambridge University formulated a set of rules governing its games. Some other clubs agreed that, indeed, some of the brutality of the sport was eliminated. But that still wasn't enough.

On October 26, 1863, representatives of eleven clubs met at Freemason's Tavern in London and formed the Football Association. But soccer did not emerge as a full-blown, modern sport from that single meeting. On the contrary, the game still had a long way to go. Some representatives did not agree with the rule prohibiting use of hands and ball-carrying, and they split off to form the Rugby Union. No provision was made for the absolute power of a referee. For years, the games were played on a kind of honor system, and it was not until after 1890 that officials took control. Up to then there were only two umpires, each taking half the

1. King Pelé is the world's
highest paid athlete.
As left inside forward
for the Santos soccer
club of Brazil, he is
outstanding on offense
and on defense

2. A soccer field in the Houston Astrodome. The short white line in the foreground is the penalty spot. Compare scale of the field with that of baseball diamond at left

In soccer, teamwork is essential. No one man ever wins a game. Each player, however, must be an expert at kicking—whether the ball is on the ground or in the air

3. *TOP:* Argentine goalkeeper and teammate fight off attacking forward.
4. *LOWER LEFT:* Center forward from West Germany launches kick.
5. *RIGHT:* In-the-air boot is tried by player at right during game at Bogota, Colombia

*A good player. can head or
kick the ball under difficult
circumstances. He can get
control of a loose ball . . .*

6. *LEFT:* Italian player heads the ball
despite opposing North Koreans.
7. *ABOVE:* Volley kick by Belgian
halfback foils an attacker. 8. *RIGHT:*
Spanish player chases a loose ball

. . . or steal the ball from an opponent or fight for possession when things get confused

9. *ABOVE:* Tackle is tried during a match in Texas. 10. *RIGHT:* Mix-up in California contest includes referee

field. Yet, infractions of the rules were surprisingly few during this time.

Those early years of the Football Association saw the emergence of the star dribblers. ("Dribbling" means moving the ball by means of the feet while keeping possession of it.) Passing had not yet become important in soccer, and most players kept the ball as long as they could. A man named R. W. S. Vidal, who played for Oxford and also for the Wanderers team, was called "the prince of dribblers." In one match he scored three goals from the kickoff in succession, dribbling all the way without a single opponent touching the ball. Another great dribbler was A. F. Kinnaird. In the 1873 finals, playing for the Wanderers, Kinnaird dribbled almost the length of the field to score against Oxford.

All sports fans have one thing in common: they constantly demand better-played games and a higher standard of excellence from their heroes. It has always been true, consequently, that teams in every sport become more skillful as time passes and individual players achieve higher goals. As the saying goes, "records are made to be broken." That is the way it was for soccer in the 1870's. Some of the games watched by rabid fans were sloppily played. The reason was obvious: teams did not have enough practice time. Soccer was an amateur sport, and the players were working men who put in long hours at a job and then played football for the sheer love of the game. Practice was haphazard at best, and that, in part, explained a lack of teamwork.

At first the teams were encouraged to train more often by a method of payment which reimbursed a player for time lost from working hours. The Association strictly forbade anyone from taking money in excess of actual expenses and wages lost. But teams were getting around that rule in a number of ways. A club could secure a job for a player as a hardware clerk or upholsterer, and the employer, who was a fan of that team, would disregard working hours as long as his "employee" practiced and made a good showing. This wasn't exactly professionalism; if anything, the player could be called a semiprofessional. This method also secured the services of a number of good players from other teams. Once, the Glasgow club came to play Yorkshire, and when the Scottish team returned home, one of their best men, Peter Andrews, remained behind. He got a job with another team, the Heeley Club, where conditions were better.

The issue of professionalism came to a head in 1884. The Preston North End team played a draw with Upton, and the game was protested by Upton because, they claimed, the Preston team had hired players. The North Enders didn't deny it, and they were not going to change either.

By that time there were too many admitted professionals playing football to outlaw them all. The Football Association was in a dreadful mess anyway. In those pre-league days, teams were not graded as they are today, and quite often a game would turn out to be a complete mismatch. For instance, Preston North End once defeated Hyde United by the outlandish score of 26–0. The Aston Villa team was so powerful and scored so many shutouts that after a while goalkeeper George Copley sat in a chair during most of the game because there wasn't very much for him to do. Perhaps half a dozen times in the course of a game some lucky opponent would get partially clear and take a shot at the Aston Villa net. Many of those attempts, however, were made from so far away that the ball just barely reached Copley's feet.

Another Association difficulty lay in the cancellation of games. Frequently, one team would fail to show up for a scheduled match. Angry fans, primed for some soccer action, were disappointed to say the least, and violently gave vent to their feelings. Something had to be done. Out-and-out professionalism was the only solution.

In 1888 William McGregor, a Scotsman, conceived the idea of a professional league with a regular schedule of games planned in advance. Fans would be sure to see the games as advertised, unless the weather was so bad that play was impossible—and no one could be blamed for that. The league was begun with twelve clubs. The 2-point-win, 1-point-draw system was established. Preston North End won that first year with a record of 18 wins, 0 losses, 4 draws. As more teams joined and the league's size grew unwieldy, a system of "promotion and relegation" was instituted. By 1898, teams were graded according to strength, so that each "division" was composed of teams capable of playing a game of soccer with equal skill. At the end of the season, the bottom two teams of an "upper" division were demoted or relegated to the next lower division, while the top two teams in that lower division were promoted to a higher division. This is the system used today.

Every sport has its players who have become almost legendary in their greatness. Ask a young American football fan about past heroes of that game and he can rattle off half a dozen before taking a breath: Knute Rockne, Jim Thorpe, Red Grange, Bronco Nagurski, Y. A. Tittle, Jimmy Brown. The heroes of soccer have similar stature, and many of them are internationally known. Billy Meredith was outstanding for 25 years, from 1895 to 1920, the greatest outside right of his time. He helped to found the Soccer Association (similar to the player associations in American sports). Stanley Matthews, "The Old Fox," dribbled and passed rings around the opposition, playing a creditable game when he was past 50. Peter Dougherty was probably the finest inside-forward of his time, a man with grace, speed, courage, and a cannon-kick in each leg. Wilf Mannion was another great one. Internationally, the stars have been Fritz Walter of West Germany, Alfredo De Stefano of Argentina, Lev Yashin of Russia, Antonio Carbajal of Mexico and many, many others.

Why, then, has soccer taken so long to become established in the United States? Did it ever have a chance to become popular? If not, then why not?

Actually, soccer has had the misfortune to be shoved aside in favor of other American sports—not just once, but many times. The game came to the shores of the United States about 1830 and seemed popular enough. The basic game appealed to the instincts of every youngster who ever walked down a paved street or dusty road kicking a rock or a stick before him. Besides, many Englishmen had migrated to America, and, as they had done everywhere, they took their beloved game with them, introducing it to other nations as an old and honored friend.

After the American Civil War, when the Football Association had already been founded in England, a number of eastern colleges decided to form an intercollegiate football association of their own. A meeting was arranged in New York City and was attended by Yale, Princeton, Columbia, and Rutgers. However, Harvard was the key school; although invited, they refused to come, preferring to stick with their own kind of football, which was referred to as the "Boston game." Perhaps, if Harvard had chosen to participate, soccer would be the established success it is in other parts of the world. But the Crimson stayed home. Their "Boston game" was somewhat similar to rugby and eventually evolved into the American form of football.

While soccer was still struggling to gain a foothold, the first professional baseball league was formed in the United States in 1871. At that time the old Cincinnati Red Stockings had fired the imagination of sports-minded people by winning 91 out of 93 games in the space of two years. In 1888 the poem "Casey At The Bat" was written and, as recited by DeWolf Hopper, was one of the outstanding theatrical presentations of its time. Against such opposition, soccer never had a chance.

Then came other sports. In 1891 basketball was invented by James Naismith, and it proved to be an instantaneous success. College football fought for a share of the limelight, as did professional football with the formation of the National Football League. How could soccer compete with America's World Series, with the professional football championship, with the Stanley Cup hockey playoffs, with the professional basketball finals?

The answer is that it can and probably will. For sometime, professional football and basketball played second fiddle in popularity to baseball—until the advent of television. Now millions watch the football games of the American and National Football Leagues; the so-called "super-bowl" is as big an attraction here in the United States as are the World Cup matches overseas. What television has done for other sports it can certainly do for soccer.

There are any number of knowledgeable sports experts and businessmen who have made this prediction. They point out that some 10,000,000 sports fans in the United States watched the World Cup matches on television. Also, good crowds have turned out to watch international exhibition matches which have been held in the United States. More than 40,000 fans saw the Santos-Milan game played in Yankee Stadium, New York City, while nearly 30,000 spectators in Los Angeles paid to watch a match between Brazil and Argentina. Perhaps they attended merely to see who King Pelé was, but for whatever reason, they did come.

In 1967 American television audiences began to see soccer matches on a regular basis. This was due, in part, to the fact that two leagues were formed: the United States Soccer Football Association and the National Professional Soccer League. The USSFA is affiliated with the Fédération Internationale de Football Association (FIFA), which is the ruling body of soccer in most organized leagues. The NPSL is not recognized and is considered a "rebel organization." According to FIFA, the rebel league does not wish to conform to established rules and regulations. The reason? Conforming can be extremely expensive.

The recognized USSFA has agreed to pay large sums of money to FIFA for franchises, plus percentages of the money taken in at the gate and additional percentages of television fees received. In addition, there is the matter of transfer fees. In the United States, ball players are bought, sold, or traded like shares of stock. Under FIFA rules, a player transfer or purchase requires payment of a fee, which can be enormous. When Luis Suarez was transferred from Barcelona to Internazionale, the fee was almost $400,-000. The Roma club had to pay a record fee of over $680,000 to get a great soccer star named Angelo Sormani. Of course, the purchasing team has to contend with the player's salary as well. Soccer players can cost a tidy sum when an entire team is considered.

Neither of the new American leagues has been looked upon with favor by teams in other countries since there weren't enough decent soccer players in the United States to form clubs for the leagues, and franchise owners had to raid the teams of other nations. But all teams are now stocked, and games are played. The crowds are not overly large, but neither are the stands empty. No one is under the delusion that soccer will prove to be an overnight success.

In fact there are people who maintain that the sport will be a long time in catching on, if indeed it ever will. Those prophets of doom give the following reasons, and even the most optimistic fan agrees that they are valid.

First, soccer is a low-scoring game. Most winning teams make one, two, or possibly three goals during a game. Americans like action and big scores. The home run is the big thing in baseball; the long scoring pass draws the yells in football. Scoring action, that's the thing.

Second, both soccer leagues in the United States have rosters of second-rate players, and they are mostly from foreign countries. Sports fans in America demand excellence, and they like to root for a home team. How can they be satisfied when the goalkeeper might come from Mexico, the inside right from West Germany, and the center forward from Uruguay? What kind of "home team" is that?

Third, soccer is competing with America's national pastime, baseball. And in every other country, soccer is a winter sport, but here the game is played in summer. Soccer players, constantly on the run, can't take summer heat. Their already poor game is bound to break down.

Soccer buffs stand firm and have ready answers for all these objections, and any others that might arise.

First, there is a game called hockey which has some similarity to soccer in that the game zooms up and down the rink and scores are just as low. The winning team in a hockey match seldom scores more than three or four goals. Also, if baseball fans like the home run, they equally adore the no-hit game.

Second, sub-par performance is accepted by fans as long as there is hope for improvement. Look at the New York Mets. Few major league baseball teams were more inept, more fumble-fingered than the Mets when they were organized. Yet New York fans took them to their hearts because of their blunders on the field. And the Shea Stadium team is improving; each year sees them play better baseball. That can happen with American soccer. In time the United States will develop its own players to compete with those from all over the world. Perhaps, some day in the distant future, the United States will win the World Cup.

Third, competition among sports goes on all the time. During the winter months, football competes with basketball and hockey. Soccer can compete with baseball, especially since soccer is played only once a week. As to the heat, human endurance can overcome that obstacle. Mile runners have cracked the 4-minute barrier in summer. Olympic competitors are pitted against each other during hot months, and they turn in record-breaking performances.

The United States has traditionally been a nation of sports-minded people. This relatively young country has learned to play and appreciate all sports—and soccer is just one more game on the schedule. As working time decreases and leisure time increases, athletics become more popular. All that is really needed for soccer's popularity to become firmly established is constant exposure.

The great game of soccer will do the rest by itself.

II

Fundamentals of Soccer

When a new player reports for basketball practice, the coach tries to find out the newcomer's basic skills. Can he pass accurately? Is he a sure-handed dribbler? Does he have a good set-shot at the basket, the ability to drive in and make a layup with either hand? Can he fake with head, shoulders, and body?

In soccer, the coach looks for good legs, stamina, and a quick mind. Can the new boy fake an opponent off balance and go around him? Does he dribble well? Is his passing accurate? Is he a team player?

Most of the fundamentals of any sport can be taught. All it takes to become good is practice—endless, hour-after-hour, day in, day out practice. One of the most quoted sentences in the world of sports was uttered by Don Hutson, a great old-time American football player: "For every pass I caught in a game, I caught a thousand in practice."

In soccer, most practice time is spent on *ball-control* and *accuracy*. The two go hand-in-hand. The most powerful kicker in the game is a useless player if he lets loose a long one that ends up in the opposition's possession. If a man keeps losing the ball when he's trying to dribble, if his passes bounce wild, if he can't take the ball away from an opponent at least part of the time, his team cannot control the ball and will not score.

KICKING

Fans of American football are accustomed to seeing those long, high, booming kicks which travel 60 yards and more on the fly. The American style kicker, especially when he is punting, is usually more interested in distance than in accuracy. Only rarely does he try to "place the ball," such as when he is trying a coffin-corner kick or wants to keep the ball away from a fast, shifty runner.

In soccer, it's not how far the ball goes but *where* it goes. All soccer coaches instill a basic idea in their players about kicking: every time the ball is kicked it is partly intended as a pass, even when the goalkeeper is attempting to clear the ball back upfield. At such times he is trying to place the ball near one of his forwards or halfbacks who is in position to continue the action.

Consequently, all soccer players learn as one of the fundamentals of kicking that the instep provides more accuracy than the toes, and the sides of the foot make for even better ball control. That doesn't mean the toes are never used for kicking a soccer ball. Far from it. The toe kick can be used with deadly effect on a direct kick from the penalty spot. With only the goalkeeper defending, the ball, traveling like a bullet, can be in the net before the poor defense man can move a muscle. Sometimes goalkeepers and full-backs use the toe kick, because they want to clear the ball into opposition territory, and the toe kick makes for greater velocity and distance. However, soccer's basic kicks are executed with either the instep or the sides of the foot.

a) The *basic instep kick* is the all-purpose kick of soccer. It is used to clear the ball out of dangerous spots, far from the goal; it is a good weapon in the long passing game.

Executing the basic instep kick involves several factors: is the ball stationary, rolling toward the kicker, rolling away from him? The technique is different in each case.

When the ball is stationary or rolling toward the kicker, he moves into kicking position by planting one foot firmly on the ground with the arch a few inches away and directly

THE BASIC INSTEP KICK

opposite the center of the ball. He keeps his head down and eyes on the ball. The kicking leg swings like a pendulum, knee bent, toe pointed down and in. When the knee is directly over the ball, the leg starts to unbend. The laces of the boot make contact with the ball just below its center, as the kicking leg snaps into the kick. The arms are held out to the sides for balance.

One of the most important parts of the instep kick is the follow through. That is what gives the kick distance and accuracy.

One glaring mistake made by many beginning soccer players is their desire to kick the ball as hard as they can. They may connect properly and execute all the movements with good form. But the ball sails harmlessly over everybody's head and often ends up bouncing uselessly across the goal line, giving the opposition possession. They might just as well roll it over to the goalkeeper.

Kicking the ball as it is rolling away requires a slightly different technique. First, the kicker has to catch up with the ball. Judging a rolling ball's speed and direction can be tricky, and the skill comes only with practice.

The nonkicking foot must be planted firmly ahead of and to the side of the ball. When it rolls into position—with the arch of the foot alongside the center of the ball which is a few inches to the side—then the kick proceeds as if the ball were stationary.

The proper timing for such a kick spells the difference between success and failure. Lashing out with the foot too soon results in a topped, flubbed kick. Trying to boot it too late can mean a missed kick.

There are all sorts of secondary factors to be considered when making a long, high instep kick. Is it a windy day?

THE VOLLEY KICK

Is the field muddy from a long rain? Is the sun bright against a cloudless sky? Wind and mud can alter the flight of a kick. Is the sun in a receiver's eyes so he can't spot the ball until it is too late?

b) **The *volley kick*** is executed while the ball is in the air, coming to the kicker either on the fly or a high bounce. Every player uses the volley kick, but it is the specialty of the fullbacks. Most often it is used to clear the ball over the head of a fast-charging opponent, and therefore the kicker does not have too much time. He must judge the ball's flight and angle, get into position, and boot it quickly.

There are two important elements in a successful volley kick. First is the position of the body. It should be leaning back slightly, with the knee of the kicking leg forward. The farther back the body leans, the higher the ball will sail when it is kicked. The second factor is the height at which ball and foot make contact. If the ball is kicked while it is still high in the air, then it will fly up high but not far away. Actually, if the body is leaning back far enough and the ball is still high, it is possible to kick it backward over the kicker's head.

The best way to make the volley kick is to have the foot connect with the ball about shin high, just as the leg is starting its upswing. The toe is pointed in and down, with the arms stretched out for balance. After the kick is made, the follow through is the same as for all long kicks.

c) The *half volley kick* is executed when the ball has taken a short bounce and is just starting to rise again. The kicker's feet and body positions are largely similar to what they would be in the general kick. But, because the ball is neither on the ground nor very high in the air, the result is usually a low line drive. Delivered with the full power of a strong leg, the half volley will zoom the ball far downfield. The half volley can also be effective in shooting for the goal.

d) The *pivot kick* can be a deadly attack weapon. It is used in corner kicks, in crossing the ball to the opposite side of the field, to fool an opponent. The pivot can be executed coming straight at the ball or from an angle. It is used by all players but is a favorite of the forwards on the attack.

The important part of this kick is the positioning of the nonkicking foot, which does the pivoting. If the pivot foot is too close to the ball, the swing of the kicking leg will be tight and cramped. If the pivot leg is too far from the ball,

the kicker has to reach out with his kicking leg. Both of those mistakes will result in a kick that has little power or accuracy.

In approaching the ball, the pivot foot should be planted firmly on the ground, about 18 to 20 inches behind and to the side of the ball. The body is leaning back and to the side. At the point of contact, the foot is turned in and pointing down. At the finish of the follow through, the body is facing in the direction the ball has been kicked.

PASSING

All kicks in soccer are at least partly designed as passes. Even the long instep kicks that send the ball behind the defense are passes, if they are delivered accurately to an open area where a teammate can reach the ball before an opponent and carry on the attack. A corner kick is a deadly pass, aimed at a teammate in front of the goal who will try to head or volley kick the ball into the net. Nobody can dribble the length of the field to score; it is the smooth teamwork of a passing game, moving the ball from man to man or man to open area that scores goals. Soccer, if it is nothing else, is a team game!

Many soccer passes are aimed in a direction different from the direction the passer is moving. The reason is simple: the defense usually shifts over to block the path of the man with the ball. This often leaves a teammate open—if the passer can see him in time. A fast, accurate crossing pass will see the attack surge ahead.

There are a number of "do's and don'ts" in passing that good players keep in mind at all times:

DO try to "lead" a receiver so that he will almost run into the pass while on the move.

DO try to pass to those open areas and make the kick accurate.

DO try to keep in mind the positions of most teammates. Knowing where friends and foes are helps in making split-second decisions.

DON'T telegraph the pass. Try to hide all intentions as long as possible. Keep the opposition guessing.

DON'T pass to a teammate who is covered. What can he do with the ball when he gets it?

DON'T execute a long pass to a teammate who is standing still. It is too easy to intercept.

DON'T kick the ball so hard that a receiver can't control it. At worst, it can bounce away to an opponent; at

best the receiver will be forced to trap the ball before
he can kick, giving the opposition that extra split second to come in and make a tackle.

The kicks that have been explained so far can all be considered instep passes. But the ball can be moved from one
teammate to another with other parts of the foot: the sides,
the sole, and the heel. These passes are short ones, deadly
accurate; they aren't going very far so they can't go wild.

The *push pass* sees the kicker approach the ball so that
the grounded foot is behind and to the side of it, at a com-
fortable distance and angle. The top of the body—hips and
shoulders—are turned away from the direction of the kick,
and the kicking leg is slightly bent at the knee, turned out-

THE PUSH PASS

ward. The body is almost over the ball, and the foot is only a couple of inches off the ground. The kicker, with a free and firm motion, thumps the ball with the inside of the foot. This type of kick is executed while the ball is on the ground.

The *lob* may also be used. Using this, the kicker passes the ball to a receiver with a kind of side-of-the-foot volley kick. The body is at an angle to the ball at the point of contact. As with the volley kick, the higher off the ground the ball is booted, the higher the ball will rise. Therefore, a lob can also be used to clear an opponent's head and reach a team-mate a short distance away. It is the knee action that sup-plies the power here.

A good, accurate pass can also be made with the outside of the foot. The ball should be slightly in front of the kicker's body. Contact is made between the ball and that part of the foot just back of the small toe. There isn't much follow through here, simply a firm movement from the hip down to the ankle.

The *sole-of-the-foot pass* is one type of footwork which will send the ball backward. This is a very deceptive ma-neuver in which the player puts his foot on the ball and with a quick move rolls it backward to a teammate behind him. The sole pass should always be executed while the ball is stationary on the ground. If the ball is moving, the kicker can lose his balance and even sprain an ankle.

The *heel pass* is the second method of backward passing. The kicker hops over the ball and taps it firmly with the heel of his boot.

Both the sole and heel passes are short ones. They can be very effective in the short passing game because the kicker acts in a way as blocker. The player receiving the pass has a man legally in front of him to screen off his actions from a defensive man.

Where kicking and passing are concerned, every player who has ever played soccer will give the same advice: practice! Practice! Practice! Soccer is a game played mostly with the feet, both offensively and defensively. If a player can't learn to use those feet with power and precision he might just as well sit on the bench or take up another sport.

The best way to practice is with a friend or teammate, passing the ball up and back while on the move. Start with short side-of-the-foot passes to warm up, get in a few heel and sole passes while weaving around each other. Then break into the pivot kicks, the volley, and half volley. Finally, more to take a breather than for any other reason, stand at opposite ends of the practice field and get off a few booming instep kicks, the kind that clear the ball 40 to 50 yards and more. Work on accuracy, trying to place the ball as near a teammate as possible.

If no friend is available, solo practice is good too. Any kind of wall that will return the ball to the kicker is useful. And, if there is no wall, kick it anyway. Run after the ball, overtake it, and kick it in the opposite direction. It builds up leg muscles and stamina.

DRIBBLING

The dribble in soccer serves the same purpose as it does in basketball. The ball is advanced by one player. If his path is blocked, he passes off; if he has a shot at the goal from close in, he takes it. A good soccer player can control the dribble about as well as his basketball counterpart. He can fake, dodge around an opponent, or dribble through him using feet instead of hands.

Dribbling is executed with the inside or outside of the foot. In a way it can be described as a kind of shortened pass, with the dribbler doing both kicking and receiving. Using the outside of his foot gives the dribbler more running speed but less ball control.

There is no hard and fast rule concerning the position of the ball in relation to the dribbler's foot. It all depends on the situation. Sometimes it's safest to "keep the ball on the toe," especially when defensive players are close and ready to move in for a tackle. In normal situations, when an opponent is an average distance away, the ball can be

DRIBBLING THE BALL

between 12 and 16 inches ahead of the dribbler. When the field is more open and the defense is loose, the ball can be pushed ahead about 4 feet or so. The most important single aspect of dribbling is keeping the ball under tight control. Every push of the ball must be measured, or it can easily end up at the feet of an opponent.

The instant a player begins to dribble he becomes a tackling target. The longer he holds on to the ball, the more time he is giving the defense to set up against him. At the same time, if he just pokes at the ball with no real intention of moving with it, defensive players will find that out too and surround any potential pass receiver. Therefore, a good dribbler knows just how long to retain possession. He will wait for an opponent to commit himself before making any other moves. And then, if he's adept enough, he'll get the ball through or around the defense man.

The first way to get around an opponent is by faking him out of position. This requires controlled use of the head, body, and feet. The dribbler can use a sudden change of pace in running speed, or a quick switch in direction, or a feint with the head, shoulders, torso, all with the idea of catching the defense man leaning the wrong way.

A fast backward pass is also effective. The dribbler makes use of the sole-of-the-foot or heel pass, then pivots and picks up the ball again, dribbling away from the charging tackler before he can reverse direction.

Dribblers who can move the ball equally well with both feet have the best advantage of all. A rapid switch in dribbling feet, a fast slant kick, and the dribbler can zigzag around his opponent.

The important thing for a player to remember in any of

these maneuvers is to keep his body between the ball and the defense man. No defender can reach the ball unless he practically runs over the offensive man, and that would be a foul.

Dribbling under the best of conditions is tricky. The dribbler has to keep his eye on the ball while kicking it, and then take a fast, between-kicks look to see where friend and foe are moving. If he takes his eye off the ball too much, he'll lose it. If he fails to look around he might run smack into the enemy.

The best way to practice dribbling is with a teammate. Each takes turns trying to fool the other's tackle attempt, using as many weapons as he has in his arsenal—the faking and change of pace, the backward kick, the inside and out- side, the foot dribbles, the switching of dribbling feet. If no friend is available, a series of obstacles can be rigged: poles or sticks in the ground, ash cans, or other objects, placed in a row at 5 yard intervals. The dribbler practices weaving through them, criss-crossing, and moving in a straight line. He can use both his feet to make these moves, practice changing feet, and use the backward kicks. The important thing is to practice.

A solid soccer attack is based on successfully mixing the pass and dribble, never allowing the opposition to get set, forcing them to commit themselves and then making counter moves. If some players on a team are weak in drib- bling, the defense has that much less to worry about and can concentrate its best efforts to break up the passing game. It works the other way as well—too much dribbling by showoff players and not enough passing cripples the chances for a goal. Soccer is a team game in every respect.

HEADING

A good part of the time during a game the soccer ball is in the air, too high to be reached by the feet no matter how high a player leaps. At those times it is very possible to head the ball, while jumping or on the ground.

People who are unfamiliar with soccer are sometimes surprised to find out how far a ball will travel when it is solidly thumped with the head. That kind of maneuver can be just as effective as an instep clearing kick, and in many respects, serves the same purpose. Heading, too, is a form of pass and demands the same accuracy as kicks and dribbles. In fact many soccer players refer to it as "kicking with the head." It isn't enough simply to get your head in front of the ball. Once contact is made, that ball should go somewhere specific.

Many athletes participating in noncontact sports such as tennis or baseball do not realize how much power lies in the neck muscles when they are properly developed. Soccer players know.

Timing is one of the most important parts of heading the ball correctly. The whole body must be coordinated to get the best effect from contact between head and ball. This is especially true when heading is executed from the top of a high leap. Judgment of height is also vital. A player should not try to head the ball that is coming in too low. If the ball is lower than chin level, forget about heading—trap it!

To head a ball while on the ground, a man gets into position facing the ball squarely. The whole body from the knees up—including legs, torso, shoulders and head—is bent back. Eyes are on the ball; the chin is up. Then, as the ball

comes in, the body snaps forward. Contact is made with the flat of the forehead, at about the hairline.

Of course, this type of heading will send the ball soaring back in the direction it came from. Many times the player wants the ball to go either left or right. In that case, at the exact moment of impact, the head twists in the desired direction, and that's where the ball will go.

When the feet are on the ground, most of the heading power comes from the body. It is the trunk and the head that execute the follow through; the neck muscles are not very important.

Heading while in the air is only slightly different. As before, the body should be lined up square to the flight of the ball. Good timing is of great importance. The player takes off on one foot to leap into the air. The arms are outstretched for balance, the head is well back. As the ball comes in the head snaps forward, and the neck muscles come into play to supply part of the power, for the body is not braced on the ground. Again, contact with the ball is made at the hairline. If the head is twisted at the moment of impact, the ball will fly off in the direction of the twist.

One of the mistakes made by beginners is the tendency to pull the neck down into the shoulders. That is wrong because the neck muscles, even in a grounded head maneuver, supply at least part of the power.

Many English players use a special drill to practice heading. It requires two soccer balls and two players. The first player throws the ball at his teammate, who heads it away in a direction called for by the thrower. No sooner is the heading executed than the other one is thrown quickly, with different directions. Not only does it supply heading practice, but it also keeps the header on the alert.

TRAPPING

The ideal pass or kick reaches the receiver about head high or rolling on the ground. It comes right to him. All he has to do is use his feet or head and the ball is advanced. But that seldom happens in soccer. Most often the ball comes in at an angle, or it is too high to be kicked and too low to be headed. The receiver has to gain possession before he can carry on. He must stop the ball, usually get into kicking or passing position, and do it quickly before an opponent can come in to take it away from him.

Trapping is done by any part of the body except the

hands and arms, whether the ball is rolling, bouncing or in the air. The smart soccer player doesn't simply trap the ball in order to stop it. Trapping can be turned into a short pass or a dribble when it's executed properly.

One of the most important parts of trapping is learning how to "ride" with the ball when it is coming in fast. Imagine this situation: a hard line-drive kick is coming right at a player about chest high. Does he just stand there and let it bounce off his body? Of course not. The ball would end up yards away, and he would have lost possession. The idea then is to take the sting out of it, cushion its speed, much the same way a catcher eases the speed of a pitcher's fastball as it thumps into his mitt. He pulls his hand back slightly at the moment of impact. It's the same principle in soccer. The player pulls back his body a little at the point where the ball will hit. The ball is kept under control. It's just a matter of timing and watching the ball at all times.

Whenever possible, a player tries to get in front of the ball, especially when it is rolling or taking short hops. That way the ball can't go through or possibly take a bad bounce and hop over his outstretched foot.

a) *Trapping with the foot* can be executed when the ball is rolling or bouncing, with the inside or outside of the foot. To trap with the inside of the foot on a rolling ball, the body should lean in the direction from which the ball is coming, with one knee bent (above the foot trapping the ball). The trap foot is a few inches off the ground and bent in, so that the shoelaces are facing the ground. As the ball comes in the foot "gives" a little, to slow it down. The foot also acts something like a weight or wedge.

When the ball is bouncing, the knee should be bent more and the foot higher off the ground. The ball should be trapped on the short hop, just as it is starting to rise.

Trapping with the outside of the foot is much harder and requires a good deal more practice. It has some advantages, for when executed correctly the player can run in almost any direction just by pivoting.

The outside-the-foot trap is usually executed with one leg "leaning across the body." The weight is still leaning in the direction the ball is coming from, on the grounded foot. The trapping foot is raised somewhat higher than it would be for an inside-the-foot trap. The body leans slightly in the direction the ball will be kicked just as the ball approaches the kicker (no use tipping off the opposition until the last possible minute). The ball is stopped, deflected slightly, the pivot executed, and the kicking or dribbling continued.

TRAPPING THE BALL

b) The *leg or thigh trap* is executed when the ball comes in on the long bounce or in the air, about waist high. The knee is bent and impact is about on the lower thigh.

c) The *chest* and *stomach traps* are both effective in causing the ball to drop at the player's feet. Both are used when the ball is coming on the fly or high bounce.

When the ball soars in on the fly, the body should be leaning backward slightly, and, at the moment of impact, the body rides with the ball to slow the ball's rebound. On the bounce, the body leans forward to cushion the ball and force it down. The arms are outstretched in all cases.

TACKLING

The tackle means different things in American football and soccer. In the United States' version of football, a tackle means to wrap the arms around a ball carrier's body and throw him to the ground. But soccer is a game of minimum body contact. So a soccer tackle is simply a maneuver to take the ball away from the man in possession or to force him to move it out of bounds, so that your team takes possession anyway. In soccer, the tackler's target isn't the man —it's the ball. Excessive contact could be called a foul.

It is just as important to know when to try for a tackle as how to do it. In some respects the situation is the same as a receiver in American football being defended by a halfback. The receiver will run straight at the defense man and suddenly cut sharply, and the defender can only try to keep pace. So it is in soccer. The dribbler knows exactly which moves he will make and when he will make them. The would-be tackler must move carefully and try to time his

TACKLING

own moves suitably. This comes with experience. In general it can be said that a tackle should be attempted only after the ball has left the foot of the dribbler, when for that split second he is not in full possession.

Making a tackle becomes much easier when the tackler knows his enemy. Is that particular dribbler weak in trying to move the ball with his left foot? Does he have the bad habit of taking his eye off the ball too long? Does he concentrate too much on the ball's position and lose track of where the defense is? Is he a "showboat," who will try to hang on to the ball too long, preferring to dribble in rather than pass off to a teammate? All these little telltale habits—and many more—help a tackler size up his opponent.

There are two basic ways to try for a tackle: from the

front or the side. A tackle attempt from the rear is too risky for all but the best and most experienced players, since it might lead to a foul or a complete miss.

a) The *front tackle* requires that the tackler get into position in front of the dribbler, blocking his forward progress. The tackler's arms are at his side (to prevent him from accidentally pushing the dribbler, which would be a foul), with his body stooped forward and knees slightly bent. The tackler is allowed to use his shoulder to block but not to knock the dribbler down. The tackling foot first blocks the ball for a fraction of a second and then knocks it away from the dribbler. If the tackle has been executed properly, the tackler should finish the play with his own body between the ball and his opponent.

b) The *side tackle* sees the tackler's feet more spread apart, but the basic technique is almost the same as for the front tackle. There is the block by the shoulder, the ball held for a moment by the tackler's foot, then the kick away. However, in the side tackle, the tackler's body is not between ball and opponent. The tackler must move around his opponent to gain possession.

Tackling is one defensive maneuver that must be practiced endlessly. There are so many things to concentrate on that sometimes even the experienced players bungle the tackle. They may back up too much while trying to get into proper position, and thus allow the ball to get nearer the goal. They may throw caution to the winds and rush in— only to be faked, feinted, and outmaneuvered by the dribbler. They lose their heads and charge in too hard. That's a foul if they knock down the man with the ball. They may not charge hard enough and be shoved to one side, politely but firmly. Their timing may be off so that they end up kicking empty air where the ball was a moment ago. They may get their own feet messed up and trip the dribbler, another foul. They can be too slow or too quick. Getting it right takes practice and more practice.

CHARGING AND OBSTRUCTING

A charge can be legal or illegal, depending on how it is done. It is not legal to go barrelling into an opponent, to knock him down, to hit him from behind, elbow him out of the way, or charge in too strongly. A charge is legal when playing to get the ball away from an opponent. Some points a player should remember about legal charging are: keep hands and arms close to the body; use the shoulder and hit

CHARGING

high; make sure to have at least one foot on the ground and that the opponent does too; play the ball, not the man.

Obstructing is really blocking without contact. Setting up in an opponent's path to allow a teammate to reach a loose ball first is one way to describe a legal obstruction. An opponent can't just run over a player—that's a foul. He has to go around. But if the player plays in his path, what can he do? This is often fine strategy when the ball is going out of bounds because of an opponent's errant kick. Obstructing the opposition from recovering in time is one way to gain possession of the ball.

THROWING IN

The throw-in occurs during a soccer game about as often as any other play. Yet it is surprising how often this seem-

THROWING IN

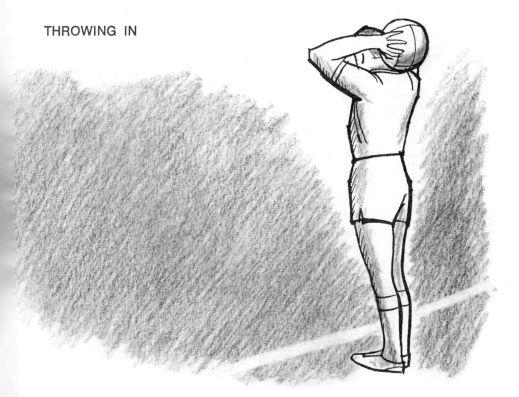

ingly simple act loses possession. A good player can throw the ball as far as he has to and put it where he wants a team-mate to pick it up.

The best way to practice is with the use of a medicine ball. It works on the same principle as a baseball player swinging a weighted bat before going up to the plate. The heavy bat makes his regulation bat seem light by compari-son. Soccer players have found this procedure helpful: prac-tice throwing the medicine ball against a wall, using the standard soccer method of over-the-head throw. Keep mov-ing back farther away from the wall. Then switch over to a soccer ball. It will feel like a feather by comparison.

These are the basic fundamentals of soccer. Constant practice will improve a player's ability in any sport and, of course, soccer is no exception.

But practice by itself isn't enough. There is no substitute for playing the game. Situations arise constantly which make the player think quickly, react almost by instinct—situations that practice alone cannot cover.

At times, mistakes happen. Every athlete makes them. Baseball's great Willie Mays has dropped his share of easy fly balls; basketball's Wilt Chamberlain has missed the open shot time and time again; American football's magnificent Gayle Sayres has fumbled more times than he cares to remember; and soccer's King Pelé has been successfully tackled by many opponents. The good players, however, keep mistakes to a minimum.

III

Laws of the Game

All team sports started out as simple games with comparatively few rules and regulations. For example, when Dr. James Naismith invented basketball in 1891, he listed only 13 rules, plus two paragraphs suggesting methods of play. Over the years new rules were introduced, some to speed up the game, others to cover situations unforeseen by Dr. Naismith. Today, basketball's rule book bulges with all sorts of technicalities. This holds true for baseball and American football.

Soccer began as a simple game, and it has remained that way. The official rule book of the United States Soccer Football Association (1967) has only 16 pages, and some of them contain diagrams and historical information. That does not mean soccer has not changed over the years, but the game has been altered far less than most other major team sports. A young boy, just beginning to learn about American football, would have to play or watch the game for a long time before he became familiar with most of its rules. Soccer can be understood by the beginner after he has watched or participated in very few games.

Some soccer rules are flexible. The size of the field, for instance, can vary by 30 yards. In fact, that is the first "Law" in soccer's rule book.

What follows is not a rule-by-rule breakdown, but a generalized explanation of the laws governing the game.

THE FIELD AND THE BALL

A soccer field is a rectangle, longer than it is wide. It is not more than 130 yards nor less than 100 yards long, and not more than 100 yards nor less than 50 yards wide. International matches use a field 110 to 120 yards long and 70-80 yards wide. In Amateur Cup play, the field can vary between 105 to 120 yards long and 60 to 80 yards wide. The field is divided by a "half-way line," and the center of the field is marked with a circle having a 10 yard radius.

The *goal area* at each end of the field is marked out in front of each goal. It is 20 yards wide and 6 yards deep into the playing field.

The *penalty area* surrounds the goal area and is 44 yards wide and 18 yards long. There is an *arc* in the middle of the penalty area which has a 10 yard radius. The *penalty spot* is a mark in the middle of the penalty area, exactly 12 yards from the middle of the goal line.

The *corner area* is a quarter circle marked out at each corner of the field. It has a radius of one yard. A small flag is at each corner of the field.

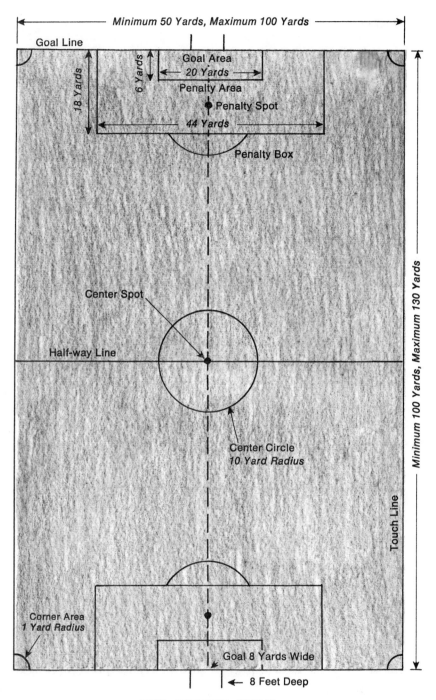

THE SOCCER FIELD

The *goals* are in the middle of each goal line and are 8 yards wide and 8 feet high. A net is attached to the posts and crossbars.

The *ball* is a leather sphere (it can be made of other materials, not harmful to the players). It is 27 to 28 inches in circumference and weighs 14 to 16 ounces. It is not changed during the game unless authorized by the referee.

EQUIPMENT

Soccer players wear a shirt or jersey, shorts, stockings, and boots. The goalkeeper wears colors which distinguish him from the other players. Players usually tape or bandage some parts of their feet for added support.

The only basic rule for players' equipment beyond what they actually wear is a general one covering "use of dangerous equipment." The greatest hazard lies in the boots. Nails, cleats, pegs, or bars that may project beyond the edges of the boots can cause serious injury. A player guilty of improper use of equipment is sent off the field by the referee and can report back into the game only when the referee is satisfied that the violations have been removed. That player can return to the game only when the ball is not in play.

NUMBER OF PLAYERS

Each team fields not more than 11 players. One of them is a goalkeeper. A player can change places with his goalkeeper but must first inform the referee.

The substitution rule can be made flexible. In some cases the rule pertains to a particular type of match play. However, in most games played under the auspices of FIFA, only two substitutions are permitted. The National Professional Soccer League permits two players and a goalkeeper to be replaced during a game.

OFFICIALS

A soccer match has one *referee* and two *linesmen*. The refree controls the game, the linesmen assist him. The referee acts as timekeeper. He can stop the game, impose penalties, caution players guilty of violations or "ungentlemanly conduct" or banish a player from the match. In assisting the referee, the linesmen indicate when the ball is not in play and which side is awarded the corner kick, goal kick, or throw-in. Linesmen carry flags which are supplied by the home team.

DURATION OF GAME

A regulation game lasts 90 minutes, in two 45-minute halves. National Junior Challenge Cup matches are divided into two 30-minute halves, according to the U.S.S.F.A. rules.

A half does not end if there is a penalty in force. If time has run out in either half and there is a penalty kick to be taken, the kick is permitted, and time is extended for it.

Allowance is made in each half for time lost due to accident or for any other time-out called by the referee.

Halftime intermission lasts 5 minutes, unless more time is agreed to by the referee.

RULES OF PLAY

Start of Play: At the beginning of a match a coin is tossed. The winner of the toss decides which end of the field a team will defend.

The game starts with the kickoff of a stationary ball at a signal from the referee. Before the kickoff, every player must be in his own half of the field. Players on the team opposing the kicker must be at least 10 yards from the ball before it is kicked. On the opening kickoff, the ball must travel at least its own circumference or it isn't in play. The kicker cannot kick the ball again until some other player, on his team or the opposing side, has also played the ball. If the player making the kickoff plays the ball again before another player has played it, then a player on the opposing team is entitled to make a kickoff from the spot where the infringement of the rule took place. A goal cannot be scored directly from a kickoff.

The kickoff is used after each goal is scored and at the start of each half. When a goal is scored, the opposing team (the team scored against) does the kicking. To open a new half, the kickoff is made by the team which did not kick off to open the match.

When a timeout is called, the ball is not in play. To start the game again, the referee drops the ball on the spot where play was halted.

Ball in and out of play: The ball is not in play when it crosses the goal line or touch line or when the game is stopped by the referee. At all other times throughout the game the ball is in play.

Scoring: A goal is scored when the ball passes over the goal line, between the goal posts, or under the crossbar. A goal cannot be scored by throwing, carrying, or forcing the ball into the net by the hands or arms of a player.

Offside: In general, being offside means that a player is nearer his opponents' goal line than the ball is when the ball is being played. There are only certain times when a player is allowed to be nearer his opponents' goal line than the ball: when a player is in his own half of the field; when two opponents are nearer their own goal than he is (one of those opponents may be the goalkeeper); when the ball is touched or was last played by an opponent; when the player receives the ball from a goal kick, a corner kick, a throw-in, or when the ball is dropped by the referee to resume play.

In the event of an offside, an opposing player gets an indirect free kick from the spot the offside took place.

Fouls and misconduct: A direct free kick is awarded to a team when a player on the opposing team is guilty of one of the following: a) kicking or trying to kick an opponent; b) tripping or trying to trip an opponent by use of legs or by stooping down in front of or behind an opponent; c) jumping at an opponent; d) charging an opponent in a "violent and dangerous manner"; e) charging an opponent from behind, unless the opponent is "obstructing"; f) striking or trying to strike an opponent; g) holding an opponent with his hand or part of his arm; h) pushing an opponent with his hand or part of his arm; i) handling, striking, or propelling the ball with his hand or arm. (This does not apply to the goalkeeper at the times when he is standing inside his penalty area.)

The direct free kick is awarded at the spot the infraction took place. However, if one of those nine infractions took place inside the penalty area, then the referee can call a penalty kick. That penalty kick can be called no matter where the ball is, as long as the player involved committed the foul inside the penalty area, and the ball was in play at the time.

An indirect free kick is awarded to a team when one of the following infringements takes place: a) playing in a manner considered dangerous by the referee, such as trying to kick the ball when it is being held by the goalkeeper; b) charging fairly, such as with the shoulder, when the ball is really not in playing distance of the players involved and they are not actually trying to play the ball; c) intentionally "obstructing" (moving between an opponent and the ball) when not playing the ball; d) charging the goalkeeper, except when he is holding the ball, or when he is obstructing an opponent, or when he has passed outside his own goal area; (e) when a goalkeeper carries the ball (takes more than four steps with it) without bouncing it on the ground.

A player can be "cautioned," with no penalty imposed, if he commits minor offenses, such as entering the field or joining his team when play has started without being allowed to do so by the referee's signal. The game can be stopped by the referee to impose such a "caution" and then started by dropping the ball on the spot where play stopped.

If a player persistently infringes the laws of the game, or shows by his actions or by his words that he disagrees with the decision of the referee, or is guilty of "ungentlemanly conduct," the referee can caution that player and also award the opposing team an indirect free kick.

A player can be ejected from the game if he persists in his misconduct after he has been cautioned, uses foul or abusive language, is guilty of serious foul play, or is guilty of violent conduct. Play is stopped to mete out that punishment, and the game is resumed by an indirect free kick by the opponents of the guilty player, at the spot where the foul took place.

Free kick and penalty kick: There are two kinds of free kicks: direct and indirect. When a player is awarded a direct kick, it will count as a goal if he can kick the ball through the goal posts and under the crossbar. An indirect kick cannot be a goal even if it does go into the net, unless the ball has been played by a player other than the kicker.

When a player is taking a direct or indirect kick from inside his own penalty area, all opposing players must stay outside the penalty area and at least 10 yards from the ball. The ball is not in play until it has cleared the penalty area. If the goalkeeper is making the kick, he must not touch it with his hands but must kick it from where the ball is resting. The ball must be kicked into play; otherwise, the kick is taken over.

When a player takes a direct or indirect kick from outside his own penalty area, all opposing players must be at least 10 yards from the ball until it is in play, unless they are standing on their own goal line between the goal posts. The ball is considered in play when it travels at least its own circumference. It must be still when a free kick is taken.

A penalty kick is taken from the penalty mark. Only two players can be inside the penalty area when a penalty kick is made: the kicker and the goalkeeper. All other players must be outside the penalty area, but within the playing field. The goalkeeper must stand on the goal line, between the goal posts, and he cannot move his feet until the ball is kicked. The kicker must kick the ball forward. He cannot

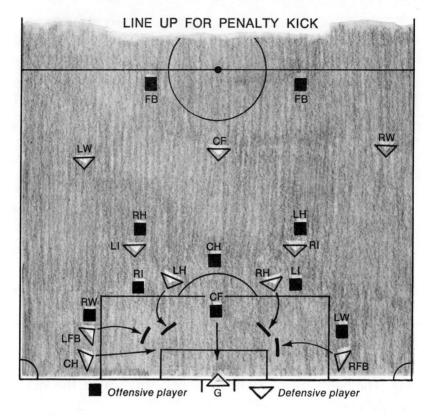

Offensive player   G   Defensive player

touch or play the ball for a second time until some other player has played the ball. The ball is in play when it has travelled its circumference. If a man on the defending team infringes those rules, the kick is taken over again. If a man on the attacking team infringes the rules, the kick is disallowed, even if a goal is scored, and the kick is done over again. If the player making the kick infringes those rules, an opposing player is awarded an indirect free kick from the spot where the infringement occured.

Throw-in: When a ball goes out of bounds, it is thrown in from the spot where it crossed the line. The throw-in is awarded to the opponents of the last player who touched the ball before it went over the line. This refers only to the

60

side lines (touch lines), not the goal lines. The thrower faces the playing field and his feet must be either on the touch line or behind it. The thrower must use both hands, and throw the ball in from behind and over his head. The moment the ball enters the field it is in play. The thrower cannot play the ball again until another player has played the ball. A goal cannot be scored by means of a throw-in. If the ball is improperly thrown in, a player on the opposing team is awarded the throw-in.

If the thrower plays the ball twice before another player has played the ball, a player from the opposing team is awarded an indirect free kick which is taken from the spot of the infringement.

Goal kick and corner kick: These two separate and different types of kicks occur when the ball crosses the goal line (but does not go through the goal posts; if it did, of course, it would mean a goal had been scored). If a player on the attacking team last played the ball before it went over the goal line, then a goal kick is awarded to the defending team. If a player on the defending team last played the ball before it went over the goal line, then a corner kick is awarded the attacking team.

A goal kick is made by the goalkeeper. The ball is placed down in that half of the goal area nearest to where it crossed the goal line. The goalkeeper cannot touch the ball with his hands before he kicks it. He cannot play the ball a second time until another player has played it. He cannot score a goal by means of a goal kick. He must kick the ball beyond the penalty area. Players of the opposing team must stay outside the penalty area while the kick is being taken.

If the kicker plays the ball again before another player

plays it, then an indirect free kick is awarded the opposing team, from the spot the infringement took place.

A goal can be scored by means of a corner kick. The ball is kicked from the quarter arc in the corner of the field nearest to the spot where the ball crossed the goal line. Players of the opposing team cannot be closer than 10 yards away from the ball until it is kicked into play. The kicker cannot play the ball again until another player has played it.

Infringement of this rule results in the award of an indirect free kick to the opposing team from the spot where the rule was broken.

IV

The Players

As the teams line up for the opening kickoff, their positions on field are a sure tipoff to their duties in the game. There are five forwards, three halfbacks, two fullbacks, and one goalkeeper. All have definite fields of responsibility. Soccer is a fast, fluid game, with the action going from end to end of the field quickly; but basically, the players must be in the right place at the right time. A player on defense who is too far out of position when the other team is attacking is leaving a gap. The other team has a better chance to score. An offensive man who is not where he is supposed to be on attack is forfeiting the opportunity for his own team to score a goal. It is the same in any sport. In American football, when a blocker leaves his post or fails to carry out an assignment, his quarterback or ball carrier will be knocked down. If a defensive back allows a receiver to get behind him by failing to be where he should be, that's inviting a long touchdown pass.

LINE UP FOR KICK OFF

Offensive player   Defensive player

THE FORWARDS

The men who usually swarm down the field to try for a goal are the line forwards. They carry the brunt of the attack, take the corner kicks, and pick up the clearing kicks from their own goalkeepers and defensive fullbacks. This group is composed of the center forward, the right inside and left inside forwards, and the outside right and outside left forwards (the latter two are also often referred to as wing men).

The forwards are the best dribblers on the team. They are also the best pass receivers. The halfbacks and fullbacks will pass off to them to start the attack going upfield.

The *center forward* can be compared, in some ways, with the quarterback in American football, especially when play is in the enemy half of the field. He ranges over the middle areas and can see both sides of the field more clearly than either of his inside forwards or wingmen. He can spot an opposing player who is out of position more quickly. If he sees the opportunity for a set play, he will give the signal to start it in motion.

Quite often the center forward acts as a decoy to pull the man defending him out of position so that a gap is opened up in the middle. This allows an inside to pour through and pick up a quick pass.

When a goalie or fullback make long clearing kicks they generally aim the ball toward the center of the field. The center forward can pick up the ball from there. He can dribble a short way or, better still, make a pass to an open spot near the sidelines where a wingman can get to it and continue the attack.

The center forward is not very active on defense. Unless special situations arise, he will seldom drift farther back into his own territory than the edge of the center circle.

Once the ball is deep inside enemy territory, he will often position himself about 6 to 8 yards from the mouth of the goal (when he does not have the ball), ready to take a pass from a teammate. He may try to kick or head the ball into the net. If the center forward does have possession in that position but is unable to take a shot, he is still set up so that a wingman can run in, take his quick pass, and try for a goal.

The *inside forwards* can be called a kind of link between their own halfbacks, the wings, and center forward. Even more than the center forward, the insides act as decoys to clear out a path up the middle. In fact, the inside forwards can and do roam around more than any other members of the team.

The inside forwards are a kind of secondary attack pair. The center forward and the outside forwards are usually farther upfield than the inside men. It is only when the attack has reached the mouth of the goal that the insides can go surging in to lend a helping hand. The reason is that they have greater defensive responsibilities than either the center forward or wingmen.

On defense, the inside forwards cover the opposing half-backs, trying to get to any clearing kicks attempted or to tackle the halfbacks before they can clear the ball.

The *outside forwards,* along with the center forward, are the lead men on the attack. On offense, the wingmen generally take up positions about 6 or 7 yards from the sideline nearest them and then dribble into enemy territory. A fast-break attack will see the wings penetrate until challenged by the opposing wingmen or halfbacks. Then a quick crossing or centering pass is executed, whereupon they drive in toward the corners of the goal to get in position to take a return pass and kick for a goal.

Quite often the wingmen will instigate the opening attack, especially if their goalie has a good strong arm. Once the goalkeeper stops a shot, he can fling the ball far over the field to a waiting wingman, who then surges into enemy territory.

The defensive assignment of the wingmen are very fluid. Sometimes a good deal depends on wind conditions. If a strong wind is blowing across the field toward one sideline, for example, the wingman on the other side must take that into consideration. He doesn't have to play so close to his own sideline. In general, wingmen help out their own halfbacks, picking up opposition drives and helping to blunt them by tackling or intercepting sideline passes.

HALFBACKS

In soccer, the halfbacks are two-way players. They are considered the first line of defense and the backup men of the offense. They must be jacks-of-all-trades, able to dribble, pass, and tackle. They team up with the wingmen on offense and the fullbacks on defense. They break up the fast-break attacks. When one team is dominating another, chances are the halfbacks on the losing side are at fault because they are not stopping drives of opposing forwards.

Perhaps more than any of the other players, halfbacks must be keen students of the game. They must have a kind of sixth sense to determine the flow of play and to get into position to meet it. They must study the attacking forwards to find out their best and weakest moves.

Halfbacks can dribble, but as a rule they prefer not to. Once an enemy drive is stopped, they must help their team mount its own attack. They are usually far back in their own half of the field. Since dribbling wastes time and allows the opposition to set up a defense, the halfback will kick out ahead of the wingmen, letting them pick up the ball. The halfbacks then trail behind, ready for a backup play.

On offense, the wing halfbacks pivot around the center half. One halfback will usually move into enemy territory, right behind the man with the ball. The center half will be in a diagonal line between that wing half and the other wing half. Thus, for instance, if the outside right forward is moving toward the enemy goal, behind him at a distance of about 10 yards will be the right halfback ready to lend a hand. Farther back and in the center of the field will be the center half. Still farther back, probably at his own end of the field, will be the other wing halfback.

On defense, all halfbacks work with the fullbacks and the forwards. They roam a good deal. They pick up the inside forwards who come in to act as decoys. Then they drop back to take care of the wingmen who are dribbling in for the close shot. They harass. They charge. They tackle.

FULLBACKS

Beginning fullbacks learn two basic fundamentals of soccer even before they step onto a field: first, don't back into the goalkeeper; second, always try to keep yourself between the man with the ball and the goal.

Fullbacks are primarily defensive players. They seldom dribble and hardly ever get into the opposition side of the field unless a special occasion has arisen—such as an all-out desperate attempt to score a goal in the closing minutes of a game. But they must be excellent volley kickers and outstanding headers. In a way, they must be the most accurate of kickers. When an enemy drive is stopped, the fullback will always clear the ball away from the goal. But he won't send out those high, soaring kicks which meander aimlessly, waiting for anybody to come and take possession. Generally, he will pass off with his kick to the forwards if he can get off a long kick to an open spot downfield, or to his halfbacks, so that they can continue with the attack.

A fullback cannot afford to be tackled once he is in possession. He's too close to the goal. Getting tackled by an inside or center forward very often leads to a score, and that is one of the primary reasons why a fullback must get rid of the ball quickly once he's got it.

Many good fullbacks, if they are fast enough, will often play up toward the center of the field when their team is on the attack near the opposition goal. That way, if they don't score and the enemy goalkeeper boots with a long clearing kick, a fullback can reach the ball first, boot it back to one of his own forwards, and then retreat back and keep watch on the game again.

Fullbacks work with the goalie mostly on defense, although they also work with the halfbacks. Working with the goalkeeper is tricky. They must try to stop all opponents from trying to get in a kick in the first place; but they must never block his line of vision. If the goalie can't see where the ball is, how can he block that bullet kick? The general rule for fullbacks is "play the man inside." Try to force him to the outside areas where, if he is going to make that kick he'll have to do it from an angle, not from square in the middle.

Soccer is like basketball in some respects, and one of them is the attempt at the "2-on-1" attack. On occasion, two forwards, working together, pile up against a lone fullback, and it's up to that single man to stop the score or to slow down the play until help can arrive. In that case the fullback should not leave the middle of the field unless he must. If he must leave, he should do so at the last possible second. He tries to play against both men, keeping closer to the man without the ball. That isn't as dangerous as it might sound, or usually there will be a pass, which will often be a lob pass up high, from the dribbler to his assist man. The fullback has a chance to get back and cover, intercept, or tackle. Fullbacks are generally big men, bigger than the others on the field. Those extra inches of height help in interceptions.

GOALKEEPER

Compared to the other players, the goalie doesn't seem to have much to do. But when the action gets heavy around the net, the bravest, most agile, and quickest thinking player is the man standing in front of the net. He knows how to dive down, leap up, use his hands, his feet, his body. He doesn't get rattled easily. He is bold, but in a careful sort of way. That means that the goalie will take chances that a teammate might not take—but only after he has quickly figured the odds, come to a decision that the action he is about to take is the best possible course, and then gone through with it. A goalkeeper has no time to weigh the pros and cons of what he does.

Goalies don't run much. They slide and shuffle as they guard the scoring gates, and are always balanced, ready to throw themselves headlong to the right or left, to "climb the ladder" and tip the scoring kick over the crossbar or to the outside.

Goalkeepers have to learn what amounts to a separate set of fundamentals since they are the only soccer players who may use hands and arms. Also, they may throw the ball with one hand, while their teammates must use both hands in the over-the-head throw-in.

Basically, there are only two ways a goalkeeper can keep the ball from going into the net: he can catch it or he can deflect it away from the net. He stops the shots either in front of the net or by going out to meet the ball.

A *ground ball kick* sees the goalkeeper stooped down in front of the net, either on one knee or squatting. He tries, whenever possible, to get in front of the ball, but if that's not possible, he stays at an angle to it. Basically, he is trying to field the ball in somewhat the same manner as a baseball fielder does. He stops the shot, cushions it with his body, and hugs the ball to his chest and stomach where nobody else can get at it. If the kick is a hard shot toward the corner of the net, the goalie will leave his feet in a headlong dive with arms outstretched. If he can get his hands on the ball and smother it into his body, fine. If not, he will deflect it out of bounds behind the goal line. Goalkeepers are not interested in being fancy about form and style. Stopping the shot is the important thing.

A *waist-high kick* is handled by getting in front of the ball with arms outstretched, hands cupped, and body balanced. As the ball comes in, the goalie takes it into his body, about stomach or chest high, "riding" with the ball to cushion its force. He must make sure to hang on to that ball! If it bounces off his body, an enemy forward is almost sure to be there to boot the rebound right back—and possibly through on the second opportunity.

A *high ball,* whether kicked or headed at the net, may be just too high to be grabbed by the goalkeeper. In that case, with a kangaroo leap, he tips the ball up and over the crossbar with the ends of his outstretched fingers. Above all, the goalie must make sure his hands are placed in such a way that the ball does not bounce back and down in front of the goal. That kind of a "soft rebound" almost always results in a score for the opposition if their forwards are alert.

A *punch* is sometimes used by the goalkeeper to deflect the ball to an open teammate. But it's dangerous. He really can't control the ball's flight, and the pass is likely to be intercepted or fly away from the spot the goalie intended. If the goalie does use that maneuver, he should hit with the knuckles, of one or both fists.

Goalies do not dribble. It's just too dangerous to fool around with the ball that close to the goal. They grab the ball and then either pass out to a teammate with a hand throw or lob a kick over the enemy players.

When a driving forward gets through the defense and moves for a shot, the goalie can't afford to stand in front of the net like a bump on a log waiting to be shot down by a bullet kick. He always goes out to meet the threat, trying to pressure the kicker into making a wild kick or to force him to commit himself. If he can only delay the forward for a few seconds, that's good enough because help will arrive. If the forward tries to dribble around him, then a dive at the ball from a distance of about 5 or 6 feet has a good chance of resulting in a save.

One thing the goalie does not do, unless it's a desperation move, is try to kick at the ball. It's too easy to miss, to have the ball deflect or hop over the outstretched leg. A goalie's first rule of thumb is to get possession. Grab that ball, and keep it away from the enemy.

Since goalkeepers can use their hands, they develop good throwing motions. A goalie's throw is a pass in the best sense of the word. He may be using a different technique than an American football quarterback, but the purpose is the same: to get the ball to an open receiver, either at his feet or just ahead of him. The throw is executed with a long, sweeping motion with the full weight of the body and the good follow through. Such throws are more accurate than clearing kicks which may go awry.

Goalies, especially, must be adaptable to all sorts of weather conditions and playing fields. Obviously, a wet ball is harder to handle. It is more slippery than a dry ball and quite apt to slither out of the hands and arms during an attempt to make the catch of a goal try. A high kick can get hung up in the wind. It can dip or sail, and must be judged accordingly. Under such conditions a goalie becomes a sort of baseball outfielder, trying to judge wind conditions and how they affect various sorts of kicks.

The greatest danger the goalie faces is the penalty kick

from the penalty spot. In about ninety percent of those cases, it's a score. The kicker is 12 yards from the goal, dead center. The goalkeeper is facing him head-on, and he cannot move a foot until the kick is made. He can't try out-guessing the kicker, can't try feinting, can't try anything. So it boils down to a case of the kicker's accuracy versus the lightning reflexes and amount of distance the goalie can cover. The goal is 24 feet wide by 8 feet high. Assume that the goalie is 6 feet tall. Assume that he can dive about 2 feet in either direction. Also, tack on another 2 feet for out-stretched arms. Thus, a fast goalie can actually cover about 20 feet of the 24 foot goal mouth. He knows that the kicker will aim for a spot close to the goal posts. The question is—which post? It helps if a goalkeeper knows a kicker's habits. Does he kick right or left? Is it usually knee high? Chest

THE GOALKEEPER

high? On a rising line into the top corner of the net? Even
if the kicker does follow the usual pattern, the goalie hasn't
been born who can move faster than a kick coming off a
man's toe. Only an outright flub or a stroke of bad luck can
prevent that kicker from scoring.

Goalies, and indeed the fullbacks and any other men
near the goal, must worry constantly about rebounds off the
posts. It's bad enough to give an opponent one shot at the
net; why give him another chance by failing to cover the
rebounds? If he has the chance, the goalie should dive at
the ball, smother it, fall on it if necessary, and risk the possibility of getting accidentally kicked in the ribs.

The goalkeepers are the final line of defense. Once they
are beaten, it's a score. Therefore, in good part, a game's
outcome depends on the goalie's reflexes, his judgment, his
courage, skill, and confidence. Without any one of those
elements, he cannot perform his job.

While the flow of play around a goal can produce any
number of situations, in general, there are certain practices
goalkeepers should follow:

They SHOULD

    1. Cover rebounds quickly.

    2. Use their hands effectively and often, in stopping
shots, in throwing, in knocking the ball away from the
net.

    3. Learn to dive accurately for the ball, to gather it
up and gain possession.

    4. Learn to judge field and weather conditions.

    5. Make it a habit to clear the ball diagonally in-
stead of into the center (at least, most of the time).

75

They should NOT

1. Let the ball bounce high in front of them. Instead, they should move out and grab the ball before it bounces.

2. Try kicking at the ball, unless it is a desperation move and there is no other way to stop it.

3. Bounce the ball prior to kicking it any more than is necessary. In wet weather especially, it can slip out of their hands.

4. Move too far from the goal. Some movement is necessary, and it must be done quickly.

5. Hesitate too long. They must make a decision quickly, then stick to it as much as possible.

V

Soccer Strategy

In American football, the difference between attack and defense is very easy to understand. The attack team takes possession of the ball, aligns itself in definite patterns, and goes through a series of set plays which may advance the ball. The defensive team also lines up in a pattern, one which is geared to stop the advance. The offensive team may lose the ball through a fumble or interception, and then the action stops while the strategy of the ball clubs is reversed. And that is all the difference in the world. There is that little pause in the collision of men while the players and spectators switch their thinking.

It's different in soccer. The ball can change from the possession of one team to another with bewildering speed. Every time that happens, the players must assume different field positions and assignments to keep up with the fast-moving play. Sometimes, even while the men are in the process of switching around, the ball changes hands again. So, quite often, any hope for executing a set play goes out the window. To a certain extent, soccer attack and defense is improvised on the spot.

That does not mean there are no plays, formations, or strategy in this free-flowing game of association football. Far from it. It does mean, however, that the players and the crowd looking on must be ready for anything. In soccer, the only thing that can be expected is the unexpected.

Another difference in the two games is a team's mental outlook. American football teams go all out to win every time, no matter where they are playing. The home field doesn't make much of a difference. In fact, most teams take special delight in travelling to another city and beating the ears off the home town club. That isn't so in soccer, at least as played in other countries. In those cases the visiting team is quite happy to settle for a tie ball game. Why? It is very difficult to explain, and perhaps it never will be understood by Americans. The whole thing is psychological; perhaps players are more inspired by home town fans and are more familiar with their own field. United States athletes point out that they too play harder before friendly fans, yet the visiting club wins a good part of the time.

Anyone studying the final scores of most soccer matches finds that they generally read 3-2, 2-1, 1-0, or a scoreless tie. That's all the proof needed to realize that soccer is primarily a defensive game. It isn't hard to figure out why. The five forwards, one wing halfback, and perhaps the center half— seven men—will move into the opposing half of the field, where they will encounter eleven players. The attacking force is outnumbered before it tries its first pass.

Still, goals are scored during a game in spite of the odds. Those players getting the goals must have mastered the basic fundamentals of soccer, including scoring patterns.

OFFENSIVE SOCCER

Basically, there are two methods of advancing the ball: the long pass and the short pass. Each has something to recommend it; each has its drawbacks.

The long pass is spectacular. It moves the ball in a hurry. Two well-placed long kicks and the ball is in the penalty area. These kicks can be high lobs that carry through the air for distance or sharp ground kicks that skid and bounce across the field. However, while long passes work well in fast-break attacks, they are risky. The high lob is in plain sight of the opposition. They know where the ball is going and have time to get under the ball. Also, when there is a stiff crosswind blowing, accuracy is impossible. The long ground kick is easier to control, but chances of finding a good sized open lane are very slim.

The short-passing game is less spectacular, but it offers better ball control. However, there are some things to be said against it. Short passes take time to advance the ball. The defense has time to get set up. Breaking through is difficult.

Obviously, the best attack is one that mixes up the long and short passes. Use the long one when the opportunity presents itself: to gain the advantage of a 3-on-2 situation or when a teammate is spotted out in the open, temporarily unguarded and in good scoring position. Use the short passes to get around closely guarding defensive men, to give the attack time to set up a play, to decoy defensive men out of the middle areas. Using both types of passes keeps the defense off balance so that they cannot play a set game against your team.

To try to diagram all the possible set plays in a single book would be useless and confusing. Many can be figured out, with variations, just as plays can be endlessly diagramed for American football. But to show just a few of the possibilities is to indicate most of them.

For the opening kickoff, the vying teams face each other and, almost immediately, the forwards of the attacking team form themselves into the basic attack pattern of soccer, the W.

The W shown is really not the one that is used all the time. The individual players can play deep to make a spread-out formation or they can play shallow closer together. The deep W is good for long passes, the shallow W for short ones. And actually, sometimes the W is erased completely, taking the form of an irregular series of curves. It all depends on the situation as to which formation is used or how far apart the men are stationed. In fact, if the flow of play worked out that way, the W might even become an M—the same formation upside down—when the inside forwards are presented with a wide-open middle area and they are unguarded.

Right behind the forwards' W come the assisting halfbacks, ready to provide help as needed. The wing halfback will always play a little further upfield on the strong side (the side on which the ball is being played), while the weak side halfback will be behind and diagonal to the center half. The fullbacks complete the picture.

Bear in mind that these are only generalized stations. All

Once a player gets control of the ball, and once he gets by the defense . . .

11. *ABOVE:* Wary of opponent, player uses side-of-the-foot maneuver. 12. *LEFT:* Attacker and defender vie for ball in a game at New York City

*. . . only the goalkeeper
stands between him and a
score. The instant a goal
kick is taken, a goalkeeper
must move into the path of
the ball*

13. *ABOVE:* Goal kick is taken in
Houston Astrodome. 14. *BELOW
LEFT:* Spanish goalkeeper faces a
threatening kicker. 15. *BELOW
RIGHT:* Goalkeeper in West Germany
falls into position

16. ABOVE: Ball is caught by alert and agile goalkeeper. 17. TOP RIGHT: Leaping goalkeeper reaches for ball in Spanish contest. 18. RIGHT: Ball is tipped over the top by Canadian goalkeeper. 19. FAR RIGHT: With a rarely seen move, goalkeeper heads the ball away

Sometimes a catch stops a scoring attempt, but only a leap will stop a high shot, get it over the net . . . or let the goalkeeper head the ball out of danger

*Sometimes a dive stops a
scoring attempt . . . even if
it means diving at the
kicker's feet*

20. ABOVE: West
German goalkeeper
dives for a save. *21.
RIGHT:* Chicago
goalkeeper goes in
for the ball. *22.
BELOW:* Halfback
from Uruguay helps
fallen goalkeeper. *23.
TOP RIGHT:* English
goalkeeper makes
desperate move. *24.
FAR RIGHT:* Ball is
already past the last
defender

*Sometimes a teammate stops
a scoring attempt. But
usually if a goalie is out of
position . . .*

or allows a kick to get by him . . .

. . . the ball flies into the net, and it's all over except the shouting

25. *LEFT:* Goalie sees ball hit his net during contest in West Germany.
26. *BELOW:* Players for New York celebrate a score

the players will shift around, depending on where the ball is. And a soccer ball can take some peculiar bounces.

As the center forward makes the move to carry the attack across the center line, in most cases the wing forwards will sweep downfield, trying to get into an open position to take a long pass. Quite possibly the center forward may try a short push pass to his inside forward, then race up the middle toward the mouth of the goal. The inside forward, in turn, might try a long pass to his speeding wing man, then he too surges ahead. Now all the forwards have moved into attack positions, into the W.

There are variations of kickoff plays, and their use depends on the positioning of the deep defensive men. For example, if the fullbacks on defense are playing too far up-field, it is possible that the racing forwards might have a chance to beat them to the goal. In that case a bit of trickery is used. The center forward might push pass to his inside man, who in turn passes back to the center half. All forwards are running into position, and a high booming kick, well placed ahead of the center forward, might put him in excellent position to kick one into the net even before the defense has taken a deep breath.

On a kickoff play, a short dribble by a back-up halfback gives the wings additional time to streak toward the goal. When defensive wings are too far toward the sidelines, they leave some center areas more open. Then a quick back pass to the halfback, a dribble up until challenged by a defensive forward, followed by a long boot to either the attacking center forward or wing forwards and the offense is in business, knocking on the door of the goal.

So the kickoff is out of the way. The ball has been worked

toward the goal. Getting it into the net requires fast timing, good footwork (or heading) plus an advantage in man-power whenever possible. That means a 3-on-2 play, or a 2-on-1. In these cases, the action is not unlike a basketball play. The extra man makes the difference. But such plays must be executed very quickly. It takes only a few seconds for another defensive player to reach the scene and equalize the odds.

Getting a man ahead of the opposition isn't always pos-sible. Soccer, as was mentioned previously, is a defensive game. There are more defenders in enemy territory than there are attackers. Besides, most play is man-for-man, and no player is likely to let his opponent get too far away. But it might be possible to fake a man out of position with

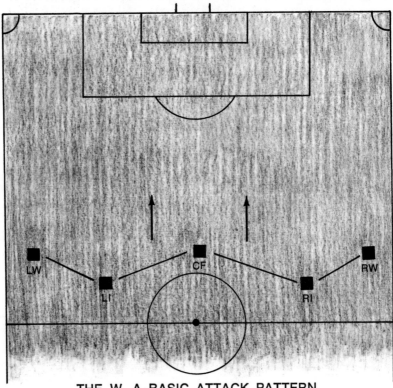

THE W, A BASIC ATTACK PATTERN

a decoy. The idea behind such a play is to open up an area, even if only momentarily. Then a quick dash into the area just vacated, a well-aimed leading pass, and a goal is very possible.

Sometimes, when an area just cannot be cleared out because the opposition refuses to fall for decoy plays, it may be possible to get in front of a defensive man, between him and the goal. Two attackers can get the ball working between them, dribbling a short way, passing off, moving in and taking return passes. Suddenly one of them puts on a burst of speed and runs by the man defending against him to take a longer leading pass. In a way, this is a variation of what basketball players call "give-and-go."

All the plays used so far have been started well within the opposition side of the field. But plays can be started by a goalkeeper or fullback with an accurate clearing kick. Then the fast-break attack can cover the length of the field. Long leading passes or relatively shorter passes keep the pressure on, depending on where the enemy's first line of defense is playing. If the defense happens to be playing very far back, or if they are playing a purely defensive game and drop back, the receiver of a clearing pass may have to dribble forward some distance. Then the long kicking game is impossible, and the short passes are used.

Of course, all these plays have numerous variations. Almost any experienced soccer player can devise a few new wrinkles, as good as any dreamed up by a veteran coach. Just as there are fundamentals in kicking, passing, and heading, so there are fundamentals to understanding soccer's basic possibilities of attack and defense.

All the plays to this point have been executed with at least some pressure on the man who set them off. The defense has moved in to force a pass or a dribble, even on the opening kickoff. On various free kicks, direct or indirect, the kicker now has time. Defensive men are yards away, and nobody is permitted to come near him until the ball is put in play.

On a direct kick, which, according to the rules, can score a goal, the kicker will find the goal stacked up with defense, especially if the shot is being taken around the penalty box. This is a time when offensive blocking and screening can be a great help.

An indirect kick from the same area might not cause a traffic jam of defensive players around the goal, since another player must touch the ball before a shot at the net can be taken. Again, the possibilities of smart screening may pay the dividend of a score.

Timing and accuracy are everything in the corner kick. A popular baseball announcer used to describe the fast, well-executed action as "a bang-bang play." This is the same in soccer. There's the kick from the corner, the split-second drive by a teammate, and then it either happens or it doesn't. A score on a smoothly worked corner kick is one of the most beautiful types of action in soccer. Sometimes the play is completed before spectators realize it.

Yet, no matter how many plays and variations are devised by expert coaches, no matter how long and hard the players are drilled in fundamentals, no matter how often a team gains possession of the ball, goals are few and far between. That's how soccer is. Kicking a football through a trained, modern defense and past an alert goalie is difficult. Perhaps it is because plays are lines drawn on paper or a blackboard, and soccer players are smart, mobile, durable human beings, capable of defending their own territory under most conditions.

Perhaps, also, that is why the closest thing in soccer to a sure score is the penalty kick. The odds are great that a kicker standing on the penalty spot will be able to pound one into the corner of the net. That is because, at that instant, soccer ceases to be a team game and becomes man-against-man, with the advantage on the side of the attacker.

The offensive plays described in this book are only a fraction of the possibilities. There are many occasions when the opportunity to use them will arise during a game. But the plays themselves are relatively unimportant. It is how the players on a team work together that counts. Do they know each other's best moves? Can they play to each other's strengths? Can they improvise an attack when a new and different situation comes up? If the players can do that, they're on a winning team. If they can't, then there are simply 11 men running around on a field. They are only going through the motions of playing soccer.

DEFENSIVE SOCCER

Once there was an army officer who won an important battle. When asked the secret of his success, he said simply, "I got there firstest with the mostest men!"

These words suggest why, in soccer, the defense is stronger than the offense. The "mostest men," all 11 of them, are already at their battle stations "firstest," ready to stop the moving W with its 5 forwards and perhaps a wing half-back and sometimes the center half in support. That would be a real "wide-open" attack, with 7 men, but even then the halfbacks would not venture too far into enemy terri-

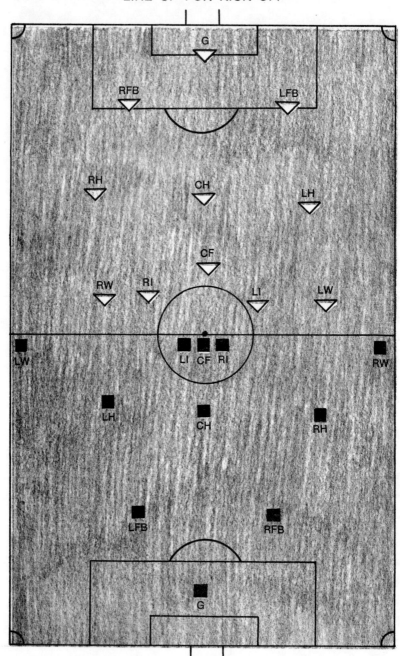

LINE UP FOR KICK OFF

tory. They don't dare! A couple of booming clearing kicks and the ball would be behind them, a situation that can spell trouble.

During some attacks, offensive players will occasionally manage to reach the mouth of the goal in the clear, and at those times someone on defense has made an error—he's let himself be feinted and decoyed out of position, or a dribbler outfoxed him, or he just plain did not keep up with his man. But there is always the goalkeeper coming out of the net to chop off the drive, give the shooter a bad angle, harass him into a wild kick, make the diving save. When the center of the field is well-covered and the defense is giving the wingmen a hard time on the sidelines, there won't be any scoring.

In soccer, the defense is a curious combination of man-to-man and zone. To see how it functions, let us return to the opening kickoff, with the same formation.

Although the defense must be basically as flexible as the attack, it can be said as a rule of thumb that halfbacks are pitted against forwards on both sides of the line.

Once the game gets going, the defense is likely to drop into a kind of formation to counter the offensive drives. There are two effective basic defenses, 4-2-4 and 4-3-3. Four forwards are up front, one forward joins a halfback in the middle, and the other halfbacks station themselves with the fullbacks. Thus the center of the field is stacked full of forwards, halfbacks, and fullbacks, while the remaining men go after the wing attackers.

Sometimes the 4-2-4 and 4-3-3 evolve into attacking formations. But that is, in a strange way, a kind of "defensive attack"—a counter-punch rather than a mounted attack. Many professional teams in international play use it. But

they are the teams who have managed to grab a lead some-
how and are content to hang on to it, or teams happy to
come out with a scoreless tie. The other team won't score,
but neither will they.

One of the fundamentals of defense is the fast, precise
switch. When an attacker's pass gets by a defensive man,
there is usually a backup man who can cover. But if the
backup man does move over, he leaves a gap—unless the
man who was beaten in the first place can race back and
plug up the hole.

If the switch is not made on time, then a 2-on-1 situation
can develop. Naturally, the defensive player, a fullback
generally, cannot cover both men at the same time. If help
is too far away to reach him in time, he must improvise. He
feints and fakes, hoping to make attackers commit themselves before he does. If he's successful, then it's back to
1-on-1 and he's got a chance for a tackle or at least might
hurry his man into a poor kick. If he is not successful, then
he goes for the man who doesn't have the ball, while the
goalie comes up to take over. Most of the time this defensive play works.

Sometimes a defense comes up against a set of very fast,
rugged, quick-passing forwards who constantly beat the
backs to the ball. If this happens, there's no use trying to
keep up with attackers. The defense must set up a stacked
zone defense, with no lanes open. The defensive forwards
take over the job of trying to break up the attack.

The toughest tests for defense come when the enemy is
awarded a free kick. The strategy that is used is determined
by the answers to three questions: is it a direct free kick;
is it an indirect free kick; where is the kick coming from?

A direct free kick taken from near the center line isn't too bad. The defense can handle it. It's rare when a kicker puts one in from 40 yards out. When the defense is set up properly, it's almost a sure thing such a long boot won't be attempted. The kicker is going to pass. However, just to be on the safe side, the stacked defense should leave a small gap in the line so that the goalie can see what's happening. There is always the possibility that the kicker might be foolish and see if it can be done.

But put that free kick attempt close in, inside the goal area, for example, and it's a different story—even if it's an indirect free kick. Nobody takes any chances. It's all hands into the mouth of the goal with no gaps left open. Then, the

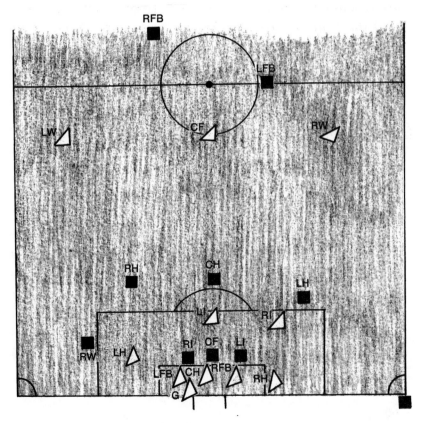

LINE UP FOR CORNER KICK

instant the kicker's foot meets the ball, charge! Remember, on an indirect free kick, the kicker can't score. Somebody else must do that, and the ball must roll at least its own circumference. This takes time. Soccer, like many sports, is a game of inches and seconds.

Of course, the toughest of all situations for the defense to swallow is the penalty kick. Nobody can help the goalkeeper; nobody can move a muscle unless that ball is kicked. But that doesn't mean the defensive players merely stand around and watch. There is always a chance the kicker will miss, that the ball will hit a goal post and rebound. There will be a scramble, and the defense has to be in position to do its share of the scrambling. The important thing for them to remember is that they must be between their opponents and the goal, set to block, screen, and charge legally. It's anybody's ball.

But penalty kicks don't happen very often because the players are usually careful. Most drives are blunted. In many instances, it's a case of the ball going harmlessly over the goal line and being put into play via a goal kick. The defense is about to switch over to offense, and both teams line up accordingly. It is almost like an opening kickoff, except that the ball is too far from the enemy goal.

That doesn't mean, however, that a fast-break attack cannot be mounted. A hard-kicking goalkeeper, with the wind at his back, plus some sneaky forwards, can spring a real threat. Then it's the former offensive team's turn to scramble, to switch, and to do it as a team. If that maneuver isn't planned long in advance, if that isn't a set play in a team's arsenal of plays, the result will be a lot of confused soccer players running around aimlessly, wondering how come they are suddenly a goal behind.

The basic attack and defense of soccer is as simple as the game itself. More than any other sport, soccer is a game of common sense and team play.

However, like other sports, it cannot be learned solely from a book. Only a coach or an instructor can point out a player's flaws, correct bad habits before they become second nature, instill spirit into men, and then drill his players until they are sharp and working smoothly on attack and defense in this international game.

Glossary
of Soccer Terms

Back-up: One player trailing behind a teammate to give assistance when needed.

Center the ball: A pass of any kind that moves the ball from the sidelines to the center of the field.

Charging: To run into an opponent, either from the sides, front, or behind. It can be legal or illegal, depending on intent and position.

Clearing kick: Kicking the ball away from one's own goal. In general it refers to a high kick that goes over an opponent's head.

Corner area: The small arc at the corner of the field from which corner kicks are taken. There are four corner areas, one at each corner of the field.

Corner kick: A direct free kick from the corner arc. When a player is the last man to touch the ball before it goes over his own goal line, his opponents are awarded a corner kick, taken from the arc closest to the spot where it went across the goal line.

Cross: A ball kicked from one side of the field to the other.

Decoy play: A play designed to draw an opponent away from a given area, to open up the gap where the opponent was covering.

Defensive end of the field: The half of the field guarded by a defending team.

Direct free kick: A free kick, usually awarded because of a personal foul. A goal may be scored on such a kick.

Dribble: Short kicks of the ball with the sides of the feet. Not a pass, for the dribbler retains possession.

First time kick: Kicking the ball without first trapping it.

Goal area: A marked area in front of each goal, 20 yards wide and 6 yards deep into the playing field.

Goal kick: An indirect free kick. When a player is the last man to touch the ball before it goes across his opponents' goal line, a goal kick is awarded his opponents. The ball is kicked from the front corner of the goal area on the side of the goal nearest where it was kicked out of bounds. The ball must be kicked beyond the penalty box, in any direction.

Goal line: The boundary line at the ends of the field.

Heading the ball: Contact between the ball and the head. It is a form of pass when executed properly.

Indirect free kick: A technical foul award. A goal cannot be scored on such a kick. It must be touched by another player.

Instep kick: A kick delivered with that part of the foot beneath the shoe laces.

Kick to a spot: Kicking the ball not directly to a player, but to an open area, where a teammate can reach it before the opposition can.

Leading pass: A pass aimed ahead of a receiver so that the ball will cross his path and can be picked up without causing the player to break stride or lose speed.

Lob: A high kick with no real power behind it. Designed to sail over the head of a defensive player.

Obstructing: Blocking out an opposing player without actually making contact.

Offside: See Chapter Three, "Laws of the Game." A player is *not* offside in his own half of the field, or on a goal kick, a corner kick, a dropped ball, or if the player was behind the ball when it it was last played.

Penalty area (box): A marked area around the goal area. It is 44 yards wide and 18 yards long. The goalie cannot use his hands outside this area.

Penalty kick: A direct free kick taken from 12 yards in front of the mouth of the goal. If a player commits a personal foul inside the penalty area, the opposing team is awarded a penalty kick.

Penalty spot: The marked spot from which a penalty kick is taken.

Ride the ball: Reduce the impact of a ball against any part of the body by "giving" or cushioning with that part of the body the ball hits.

Save: Stop a shot at the net taken by an opposing player.

Switch: When one player takes over the spot normally covered by a teammate, and the teammate in turn covers the first player's area. A game is not stopped to allow for switches. Players usually make them smoothly and with little hesitation.

Tackle: Gain possession of the ball by stealing it away from an opposing player who has been dribbling or is about to kick it.

Throw-in: When the ball goes across the touch line, possession is awarded to the opponents of the last player to touch the ball. The throw-in must be made by both hands, using an over-the-head motion.

Touch line: The sideline marking the boundary of the field on each side.

Trapping: Stopping the ball's flight with any part of the body except the hands and arms. Once the ball is trapped it drops to the ground, and the player tries to gain possession for a pass or dribble.